G. HASLBECK   D. WARDALE

MIT GEÖFFNETEM REGLER
TEIL III: ASIEN (Band 1)

STEAM ON 4 CONTINENTS
PART III: ASIA (Vol. 1)

von Günter Haslbeck und David Wardale

mit Beiträgen von

Hugh Ballantyne
Donald Brooks
B. R. Chennell
Keith R. Chester
Christian Eilers
Wolfgang Eilers
I. C. Foot
Werner Fritthum
Robin Garn

Thomas A. Markert
Ray Marsh
Hans Münch
Günter Oczko
Kurt Otto
Bernd Schurade
Robert Stevens
Irene M. Wardale

IMPRESSUM

Veröffentlicht von Verlag Günter Haslbeck
Heydenreichstr. 3, 8400 Regensburg
Germany

Auslieferung: Westendstr. 14
            8400 Regensburg

1. Auflage 1991

ISBN 3-925314-02-4

Copyright 1991, David Wardale, Günter Haslbeck

Lithographie und Satz: Rotaplan, Regensburg

Druck: Printers srl.
I-38100 - Trento · Lamar di Gardolo

Rechts: An einem Aprilnachmittag 1981 befördert eine PJKA CC50 1'CC Mallet den 12.50h Zug von Cibatu nach Cikajang über eine Brücke zwischen Banjarsari und Bayongbong in Java. Die Reisenden können die wilden Wolkenformationen genauso genießen wie der glückliche Photograph. (DB)

Right: On an April afternoon in 1981 a PJKA CC50 class 2-6-6-0 Mallet heads the 12.50 Cibatu – Cikajang train across a bridge between Banjarsari and Bayongbong in Java. Those on board the train have a perfect view of the drama enacted in the sky over them by immense stormclouds. (Photograph DB).

Inhalt / Contents

Einführung

Asien ist heute der einzige Kontinent mit einem nennenswerten Dampfbetrieb. Zu Beginn der 80er Jahre konzentrierten sich in Indien und China, den beiden Ländern mit den meisten Dampflokomotiven, zusammen etwa 70 % des Weltbestandes an aktiven Dampflokomotiven. Mit dem Rückgang der Dampfleistungen in anderen Ländern vergrößert sich dieser Prozentsatz noch.

Die für die Wettbewerbsfähigkeit notwendigen Voraussetzungen, nämlich billiger einheimischer Brennstoff und ein Überangebot an billigen Arbeitskräften, sind in vielen Ländern Asiens gegeben. Hinzu kommt, daß wegen der weitverbreiteten Armut das Kapital für den Kauf neuer Lokomotiven oft knapp war. In dieser Situation blieb oft keine andere Wahl als die Dampflokomotive, da sie bei vergleichsweise geringen Anschaffungskosten hohe Zugkraft entwickelte. Dies gilt insbesondere für Indien und China, wo Dampflokomotiven in eigener Fertigung, mit einem minimalen Anteil an importierten Teilen, hergestellt wurden. Für die meisten Eisenbahnen in Asien reichte die Zugkraft von Dampflokomotiven aus. Ihre Unverwüstlichkeit kam den häufig schlecht ausgebildeten Arbeitskräften entgegen, so daß Dampflokomotiven gerne als Maschinen angesehen wurden, deren Funktionsfähigkeit unter oft primitiven Verhältnissen als bewiesen galt.

Obwohl diese Umstände den verbreiteten Einsatz von Dampflokomotiven in Asien länger hinausgezögert haben als in anderen Kontinenten, so fährt auch hier die Dampflok im Gegenwind. Auf den großen Bahnnetzen kann derzeit nur noch in China die Dampftraktion den 1. Rang behaupten, mit einem raschen Rückgang des prozentualen Anteils am Gesamtverkehr ist jedoch zu rechnen. Mehrere tausend Dampflokomotiven stehen in Indien noch im Einsatz, diese bespannen jedoch zunehmend weniger wichtige Züge. Schnellzüge und schwere Güterzüge sind die Domäne von Diesel- und elektrischen Lokomotiven. Auf den Staatsbahnen Japans und Indonesiens kam der Dampfbetrieb in den 70er bzw. 80er Jahren zum Erliegen, während bei anderen wichtigen Nutzern (z. B. UdSSR, Türkei, Pakistan) im gleichen Zeitraum ein drastischer Rückgang zu verzeichnen war. Nichtsdestoweniger werden in einigen Regionen Asiens Züge auch ins 21. Jahrhundert dampfen, ja vielleicht sogar noch am 200. Jahrestag der Inbetriebnahme der 1. öffentlichen Eisenbahn in Großbritannien.

Wegen der Riesenauswahl an Fotos wird der asiatische Teil der Buchreihe „Mit Geöffnetem Regler" in zwei Bänden produziert. Das vorliegende Buch beinhaltet die Länder Türkei, Pakistan, Indien, Indonesien und einige andere, wogegen der später erscheinende Band IV China als Schwerpunkt haben wird. Leider fehlt die UdSSR, aber dort waren die Fotografierbedingungen alles andere als günstig für den fotografischen Stil dieser Buchreihe.

Introduction

Asia was the last continent to have a fairly widespread use of steam traction. At the start of the 1980's India and China, by then the world's two biggest steam users, together possessed some 70 % of the world-wide active steam stock, and this fraction tended to increase as other countries diminished their steam operations.

The usual factors necessary for steam to be competitive, i. e. cheap indigenous fuel and abundant cheap labour, are present in many Asian countries. In addition much of the continent is not highly developed economically, so that funds for purchasing new locomotives have often been limited. In this situation the type of locomotive that can produce the highest power for a given initial cost has frequently to be the first choice. As a rule this type has been steam, especially where it could be built locally with the minimum of imported parts, as in India and China. On most Asian railways steam has provided sufficient tractive capacity to move the traffic offered, and its apparant simplicity has suited the mostly unsophisticated workforces, resulting in a tendency to view steam as something familiar which has proved workable in operating conditions that are often rather primitive.

Although these circumstances have allowed steam to play a major role for longer in Asia than elsewhere, even this continent has not escaped the winds of change. At the time of writing, of all the large systems the Chinese Railways makes the greatest use of steam locomotives, but the share of the total traffic worked by steam there is falling rapidly and steam is no longer the dominant type of traction. A few thousand steam locomotives remain serviceable in India, but their operation is increasingly confined to relatively minor duties, most express passenger and heavy freight traffic having been taken over by diesel and electric traction. The state railway systems in Japan and Indonesia phased steam out during the 1970's and 1980's respectively, and other major users (e. g. USSR, Turkey and Pakistan) greatly curtailed their steam operations during the same period. Despite this it is probable that steam will be hauling trains into the 21st century in some parts of Asia.

Because of the quantity of suitable photographs available, the Asian part of Steam On 4 Continents is being produced as two volumes. The present book, Part III of the series, covers Turkey, Pakistan, India and Indonesia plus some minor countries; Part IV, to be published later, will concentrate on China. A regrettable omission is the USSR, at one time the biggest steam user of all. Unfortunately conditions there have not been completely favourable for obtaining the type of photographs used in this series.

Türkei

Die Türkei hat Landanteile in Europa und in Asien. 95 % der Landfläche werden dem asiatischen Kontinent zugerechnet, ebenso liegt der weitaus größte Teil seiner Eisenbahnstrecken östlich des Bosporus, so daß die Türkei dem Asienteil dieser Buchreihe zugeordnet wurde.

Geographisch besteht das Land größtenteils aus der anatolischen Hochfläche, mit einer Durchschnittshöhe von ca. 1000 m im Westen bis über 2000 m im Osten. Viele Hügelketten und Gebirgszüge steigen darüber hinaus. Im Landesinneren weist das Klima stark kontinentale Merkmale auf, mit heißen, trockenen Sommern, die von rauhen, oft schneereichen Wintern abgelöst werden. Die Landoberfläche bietet somit genug Schwierigkeiten für den Bau und Betrieb von Eisenbahnstrecken, insbesondere für diejenigen, die den großen Höhenunterschied vom Küstenbereich ins Landesinnere bewältigen müssen. Dies ist sicherlich einer der Gründe für das weitmaschige Streckennetz der Türkei. Bis heute gibt es eine Anzahl recht großer Städte ohne Bahnverbindung. Der Enthusiast wird jedoch durch die begeisternde Anlage der bestehenden Strecken mehr als entschädigt. Die meisten für Gebirgsbahnen typischen Merkmale, z. B. steile Rampen, enge Krümmungen, in Felswände gehauene Trassen, finstere Tunnel und hohe Viadukte lassen sich in der Türkei bestaunen.

Fast alle von den Türkischen Staatsbahnen (TCDD) seit ihrer Gründung 1927 in Dienst gestellten Dampflokomotiven waren vier- oder fünffach gekuppelt, besonders geeignet für den Einsatz auf Steilstrecken. Dominant war die Achsfolge 1'E, von der zwischen 1937 und 1955 insgesamt 355 Maschinen von verschiedenen Herstellern in Deutschland, Österreich, Großbritannien, der Tschechoslowakei und in Nordamerika geliefert wurden. 166 dieser Lokomotiven basierten auf einem erstmals von Henschel 1937 ausgelieferten Design, bekannt geworden als Standard 1'E, eine robuste Zweizylinderlok, mit einem guten mechanischen und thermodynamischen Design. Dieser Loktyp scheint die nützlichste und beliebteste Baureihe gewesen zu sein. Die beiden letzten von den TCDD in Dienst gestellten Dampflokomotiven, die in deren eigenen Werkstätten 1961 entstanden, basierten folglich auf diesem Design. Eine ebenfalls wohlbekannte 1'E Baureihe ist die 56.3xx, von der zwischen 1947 und 1949 insgesamt 88 Maschinen von Vulcan, USA, gebaut wurden. Üblicherweise wurden sie als „Skyliner" bezeichnet, da die über die Kesseloberseite gezogene Verkleidung ihnen ein unverwechselbares Äußeres gab. Dadurch sind sie gewissermaßen zu einem Symbol für den Dampfbetrieb in der Türkei geworden.

Zu den 1'E kamen noch viele andere interessante Loktypen, ja, die Baureihenvielfalt war geradezu ein Kennzeichen für die TCDD bis in die jüngste Zeit. Diese Tatsache, verbunden mit der wilden, großartigen Landschaft, durch die die Züge fuhren, machten die Türkei zu einem El Dorado für Eisenbahnfreunde in den 70er und frühen 80er Jahren, bevor die Dieseltraktion alle Streckendienste übernahm.

Turkey

Turkey forms a bridge between Europe and Asia. However 95 % of its land mass and almost all its railways lie on the Asian side of the Bosporus, making it essentially an Asian country for the purposes of this series.

Topographically the bulk of Turkey consists of the Anatolian plateau which varies in altitude from about 1000 metres above sea level in the west of the country to over 2000 metres in the east. Rising from this plateau are many ranges of hills and mountains, and the area is also one of climatic extremes, hot summers being followed by frigid winters with heavy snowfalls. The terrain is therefore a difficult one through which to build and operate railways, especially where they must make the arduous climbs inland from the coastal cities. This probably explains why Turkey's railway network is rather sparse; even today there are many quite large towns which have no railway connections. However from the enthusiasts' viewpoint this was adequately compensated by the often spectacular nature of those lines which were built. Most of the features associated with mountain railways, such as severe grades and curvature, lines perched on ledges cut into mountainsides, tunnels, viaducts and so on, are to be found in Turkey.

Almost all steam locomotives acquired by the Turkish State Railways (TCDD) since its formation in 1927 have been 8 or 10-coupled types suited for operation on steeply graded lines (mainline ruling grades are as steep as 2,5 %). The 2-10-0 was the dominant type, with 355 locomotives of this wheel arrangement being supplied by builders from Germany, Austria, Britain, Czechoslovakia and America over the period 1937–55. Of these, 166 were to a design first supplied by Henschel in 1937 which has become known as the "standard" 2-10-0. A straightforward 2-cylinder machine of good all-round mechanical and thermodynamical design, it seems to have been the most useful and popular of Turkey's steam locomotives. Appropriately the last two steam locomotives put into service by the TCDD, both built in its own workshops in 1961, were basically to this design. Another well-known 2-10-0 class was the 56.3XX series of 88 locomotives built by Vulcan, USA, in 1947–49. Popularly termed the "skyliners" because of the casings mounted along the full length of their boilers, the distinctive appearance of these locomotives made them something of a symbol of Turkish steam.

Many other interesting classes operated alongside the 2-10-0's: indeed a feature of the TCDD until fairly late in the steam era was the large variety of types in service relative to the limited total stock of locomotives. This, together with the rugged grandeur of the scenery through which the locomotives worked, made Turkey one of the best countries for the steam enthusiast until the mid – 1980's when dieselization almost eliminated mainline steam workings.

Die Steilrampe von Balikesir nach Yeniköy, von wo aus es dann in die Hafenstadt Bandirma wieder abwärts geht, machte bei schweren Zügen 3 bis 4 Lokomotiven erforderlich. Zu sehen sind drei 1'E mit einem Erzzug auf der anstrengenden Bergfahrt zwischen Balikesir und Yeniköy, März 1984.

The grade on the northbound climb from Balikesir was steep enough to require three or four locomotives on heavy trains heading towards Bandirma. Here three 2-10-0's on a mineral train slog uphill to the summit near Yeniköy where the banking section ends, March 1984.

KRC

Der schwache Oberbau auf der Strecke Izmir – Uşak – Afyon erforderte den Einsatz der 57.0 1'E1' sowie der 56.5 1'E (ehemalige DR Kriegslok). In dieser Aufnahme aus dem Dezember 1984 sieht man eine 56.5 vor dem 7.05h GmP Afyon – Alaşehir bei Balmahmut im ersten Sonnenlicht glänzen.

Due to axleload limitations traction on the Izmir – Uşak – Afyon line was restricted to the 57.XXX class 2-10-2's and the 56.5XX series 2-10-0's (ex-DR "Kriegslok" design). In this December 1984 view one of the latter class heading the 07.05 Afyon – Alaşehir mixed near Balmahmut glints in the light of the rising sun.

GH

56.530 kämpft sich im April 1984 mit dem 7.05h GmP von Afyon nach Alaşehir durch einen bei Dumlupinar wütenden Schneesturm. Dumlupinar ist der höchste Punkt der Strecke Izmir – Afyon.

GH

In April 1984 2-10-0 no. 56.530 is caught in a spring snowstorm as it works the 07.05 Afyon – Alaşehir mixed close to Dumlupinar, the highest point on the line between Izmir and Afyon.

Zwei 57er 1'E1' stampfen die Steigung nach Uşak mit dem GmP von Izmir nach Kurtalan hinauf. Die Aufnahme stammt aus dem April 1984.

Two 57.XXX class 2-10-2's head up the grade to Uşak with the 08.15 Izmir – Kurtalan train during April 1984.

GH

Mit Steigungen bis 25⁰/₀₀ verlangte die Strecke Izmir – Uşak – Afyon häufig Vorspannleistungen. Die Dampffahne zweier 56.5 Kriegsloks bleibt in der kalten und stillen Luft stehen, als sie den 8.15h Zug von Izmir nach Kurtalan aus Uşak heraus beschleunigen, April 1984.

GH

The 2,5% ruling grade on the Izmir – Uşak – Afyon line necessitated frequent doubleheading. Here two 56.5XX class 2-10-0's leave their steam trails hanging in the cold humid air as they haul the 08.15 Izmir – Kurtalan train away from Uşak during April 1984.

Der tägliche Zug Izmir – Kurtalan eilt im Dezember 1984 mit seiner 56.5 1'E zwischen Inay und Ovaköy in die hereinbrechende Nacht. Die aus dem Kamin herausgeschleuderten Funken heben sich deutlich gegen die dunklen Regenwolken ab.

In December 1984 a 56.5XX 2-10-0 heads into the darkness between Inay and Ovaköy with the daily Izmir – Kurtalan train as gathering stormclouds close in on the world and accelerate the coming of nighttime. Sparks from the locomotive's chimney are clearly visible.

GH

Oben: *Ein Spiel aus Licht und Schatten! Zwei 1'E Kriegsloks stürmen mit dem 6.10h GmP Alaşehir – Afyon an Ovaköy vorbei. Gleich wird die letzte Steigung vor Uşak gemeistert sein, Januar 1985.*

Links: *Der Tag geht zu Ende und ein Höhenunterschied von 700 m ist schon fast geschafft, als 56.549 sich im Dezember 1984 mit dem 8.15h Zug Izmir – Kurtalan der Station Inay, kurz vor Uşak gelegen, nähert.*

Above: *Light and dark compete for the sky as two 56.5XX series 2-10-0's on the 06.10 Alaşehir – Afyon mixed storm past Ovaköy on the last part of the climb to Uşak, January 1985.*

Left: *The last rays of the setting sun illuminate "Kriegslok" 2-10-0 no. 56.549 heading the 08.15 Izmir – Kurtalan train near Inay on the 700 metre climb between Alaşehir and Uşak, December 1984.*

Beide GH

HB

Oben: *Kurz vor dem Tunnel bei Güneyköy stampfen 56.524 und 56.522 mit dem täglichen GmP Alaşehir – Afyon bergan, September 1985.*

Rechts: *Rotgoldenes Abendlicht und ein Grollen in der Ferne! Das Grasland am Fuß des Akdağ erbebt, als sich 56.518 mit ihrem glühenden Scheinwerfer in die hereinbrechende Nacht tastet. Diese stimmungsreiche Aufnahme der 1'E mit ihrem Güterzug von Afyon nach Denizli entstand im September 1984 bei Sütlaç.*

Above: *2-10-0's 56.524 and 56.522 pound upgrade towards the tunnel at Güneyköy with the daily Alaşehir – Afyon mixed, September 1985.*

Right: *A vision of a train set in a golden landscape. As the grasslands at the foot of the Akdağ reflect the rich colour of a brilliant setting sun, the glowing headlight of a distant locomotive already anticipates the darkness of the coming night. This evocative photograph of 2-10-0 no. 56.518 on an Afyon – Denizli freight was taken near Sütlaç in September 1984.*

Burdur-System (Von Dinar nach Burdur, Isparta und Eğridir). Die Dampffahnen mischen sich mit dem Frühdunst, als ein GmP nach Gümüşgün mit seiner 55.0 aus Bozanönü ausfährt und eine weitere Lok dahinter rangiert, April 1984.

The Burdur system (Dinar to Burdur, Isparta & Eğridir). Steam trails lie in the hazy valley near Bozanönü as an early morning train to Gümüsgün headed by a 55.0 class 0-10-0 is followed by a light engine, April 1984.

GH

Bis Mitte der 80er Jahre wurden fast alle Züge auf dem Burdur-System von den TCDD Baureihen 44.0 beziehungsweise 55.0 (basierend auf den preußischen G8 beziehungsweise G10) gezogen. Zu sehen ist die Silhouette des E-Kupplers 55.013 mit dem 18.30h Zug nach Eğridir nahe dem Scheitelpunkt der Steigung zwischen Dinar und Karakuyu. Die Sonne war an diesem wolkenlosen Septemberabend 1984 bereits untergegangen.

As late as the mid-1980's most traffic on the Burdur system was worked by locomotives of Prussian Railway G8 and G10 designs (TCDD classes 44.0 and 55.0 respectively). In this view 0-10-0 no. 55.013 approaching the summit of the climb to Karakuyu with the 18.30 Dinar – Eğridir passenger train is seen silhouetted against a cloudless sky shortly after sunset on a September evening in 1984.

CE

Die D-Kuppler 44.055 und 44.017 ziehen den 18.20h Zug Eğridir – Dinar im April 1983 gemeinsam über den Steilabschnitt am Eğridir-See. Der Zug war an diesem Tag auf 7 Wagen verstärkt worden, da er zusätzlich Truppen transportieren mußte, und benötigte deshalb eine Vorspannlokomotive.

GH

0-8-0's nos. 44.055 and 44.017 doubleheading the 18.20 Eğridir – Dinar train climb past Lake Eğridir in April 1983. Normally singleheaded, the train on this occasion had a number of extra coaches added to accomodate troops, necessitating the use of two locomotives.

„Skyliner" 56.385 macht im Januar 1985 kurz Halt in Eskipazar, bevor es mit dem Güterzug Karabük – Çankiri weiter in die Berge geht. Der Eindruck immenser Kraft, hervorgerufen durch die wuchtige Frontpartie, trügt vermutlich, da das Design der Frontpartie bei amerikanischen Dampflokomotiven allgemein nicht optimal war.

"Skyliner" 2-10-0 no. 56.385 pauses in Eskipazar during its journey from Karabük to Çankiri with a freight train in January 1985. Unfortunately, due mainly to the sub-optimum front-end design typical of American practice, the impression of high power suggested by the compact ruggedness of these locomotives was probably illusory.

GH

1'E Nr. 56.331 nimmt mit Elan die 18 %₀ Steigung vor Eskipazar mit ihrem 6.30h Güterzug von Karabük nach Çankiri, Mai 1984.

WF

2-10-0 no. 56.331 makes a characteristically spirited ascent of the 1,8 % grade on the climb to Eskipazar with the 06.30 Karabük – Çankiri freight, May 1984.

Bergan gegen den Sturm! Zwischen den schwarzen Wänden eines Einschnitts bei Sumuçak fährt ein „Skyliner" mit seinem Güterzug nach Çankiri einem düsteren Januarabend 1985 entgegen.

Framed by the dark walls of a cutting near Sumuçak, a "Skyliner" 2-10-0 battles with wind and grade as it heads a Çankiri – bound freight into the twilight on a stormy evening during January 1985.

GH

KRC

Oben: Im Bw Irmak wird der Abdampf der 56.304 durch den Scheinwerfer einer anderen Lokomotive feurig angestrahlt, April 1977.

Rechts: Die Weichen in Richtung Abstellgleis sind für die 1'E Nr. 56.385 schon gestellt, als sie mit ihrem Güterzug von Karabük nach Çankiri entlang eines Friedhofs bei Kurşunlu bergab rollt, Januar 1985.

Above: Escaping steam illuminated by the headlight of another locomotive forms a fiery-looking glow around 2-10-0 no. 56.304 standing at Irmak depot, April 1977.

Right: Nearing the end of its own life, 2-10-0 no. 56.385 on a Karabük – Çankiri freight rolls downhill near Kurşunlu through a scene full of ominous symbolism for the fate of steam, January 1985.

Im schmutzigen Alltagsgewand präsentiert sich die 56.363 mit ihrem Kohlezug in das Kraftwerk Işıkveren bei Çatalağzi. Das Ende des Dampfbetriebs war im Juni 1985 nahe, als diese Aufnahme in Zonguldak entstand.

In June 1985, during the waning days of steam in this area, a grimy 56.363 storms out of Zonguldak with a coal train for the Işıkveren power station near Çatalağzi.

WF

Die Felswände beben, als 1'E Nr. 56.328 mit voller Kraft am Silvestertag 1984 bei Tuney mit ihrem Güterzug von Cankiri nach Irmak donnert.

The cutting walls vibrate as "Skyliner" 2-10-0 no. 56.328 blasts uphill near Tuney with a Çankiri – Irmak freight on New Year's Eve 1984.

GH

Schwärzer geht's nicht! Die ölgefeuerte 1'E Nr. 56.052 verqualmt mit einem „World Steam" Sonderzug im August 1989 die Umgebung von Pinarli auf der Strecke von Malatya nach Elazığ.

WE

The densest of black smoke pours from the chimney of oil-fired 2-10-0 no. 56.052 seen here climbing near Pinarli on the Malatya – Elazığ section with a special train organised by "World Steam" during August 1989.

Einen hübschen Anblick bietet die „Middle East" 1'D1' Nr. 46.235 (Alco 1942) mit ihrem „World Steam" Sonderzug im September 1986 auf einem Viadukt bei Gölbaşı auf der Strecke von Adana nach Malatya.

Oil – fired "Middle East" class 2-8-2 no. 46.235 (Alco 1942) makes a fine sight as it crosses a viaduct near Gölbaşı on the Adana – Malatya section with a "World Steam" railtour train, September 1986.

BS

Anfang 1985 wurden die meisten Züge auf der Strecke von Samsun am Schwarzen Meer nach Sivas noch von den auf preußischem Design beruhenden G8² gezogen. Zwei solche 1'D Maschinen kämpfen sich im März 1985 langsam durch die zweifache Hufeisenkurve bei Ladik, wo die lange Steigung von der Küste her endet.

IMW

The 45.0 class 2-8-0's, based on the Prussian Railway G8² design, still worked most trains on the Samsun – Sivas line during early 1985. This photograph taken in March of that year shows two of these locomotives struggling to keep a southbound freight moving on the double horseshoe curve at Ladik, near the summit of the long climb from the Black Sea coast.

Entlang den dunklen Fluten des Schwarzen Meeres fährt eine 45.0 mit ihrem nachmittäglichen Personenzug von Samsun nach Azot, Februar 1986.

A 45.0 class 2-8-0 heads an afternoon Samsun – Azot passenger train past the dark waters of the aptly named Black Sea, February 1986.

TAM

Eine Standard 1'E stampft das Euphrat-Tal hinauf, nachdem sie kurz zuvor mit dem 5.11h Güterzug nach Erzurum aus Erzincan abgefahren war, April 1985.

DW

A standard 2-10-0 pounds up the Euphrates valley soon after leaving Erzincan with the 05.11 freight to Erzurum, April 1985.

Die 1'E Nr. 56.119, Zuglok des 6.45h GmP von Divriği nach Erzincan, durchfährt im April 1985 die wenige Kilometer westlich von Erzincan gelegene Schlucht.

2-10-0 no. 56.119 at the head of the 06.45 Divriği – Erzincan mixed passes through a gorge just west of Erzincan during April 1985.

DW

„Kriegslok" Nr. 56.543 dampft mit den 2 Wagen des 5.15h Zuges von Karasu nach Erzurum durch die offene Landschaft Anatoliens, April 1985.

DW

"Kriegslok" 2-10-0 no. 56.543 ambles through a typically massive Turkish landscape west of Erzurum with the 2-coach 05.15 Karasu-Erzurum local train, April 1985.

Die Strecke Erzurum – Kars führt bis auf etwa 2300 m über dem Meer bei Yeniköy. Zu sehen ist die 1'E Nr. 56.539, die den 5.33h GmP von Erzurum nach Kars im Schrittempo durch die wild-einsame Berglandschaft zwischen Topdaği und Soğanlı befördert, Februar 1984.

The Erzurum – Kars line ascends to some 2300 metres above sea level after Yeniköy and passes through some spectacular scenery. Here 2-10-0 no. 56.539 slows to a walking pace as it struggles upgrade through the desolate mountains between Topdaği and Soğanlı with the 05.33 Erzurum – Kars mixed in February 1984.

GO

Rechts: *Die Standard 1'E Nr. 56.123 bringt den kurzen 5.18h Horasan – Erzurum Personenzug bei Köprüköy in Schwung, März 1986.*

Links: *Der dunkle Zug und der schwarze Rauch bilden einen schönen Kontrast zu den blendend weißen Schneebergen. Das Foto zeigt die 56.143 im Anstieg auf Soğanlı im April 1985.*

Right: *Standard 2-10-0 no. 56.123 accelerates the short 05.18 Horasan – Erzurum local train away from Köprüköy station, March 1986.*

Left: *The 05.33 Erzurum – Kars mixed train hauled by standard 2-10-0 no. 56.143 climbs to Soğanlı during April 1985; the dark form of the train and the smoky exhaust from the locomotive contrast with the dazzling whiteness of the snow-covered slopes behind.*

RS

Die Sturmwolken lassen weitere Schneefälle in der Umgebung von Soğanlı erahnen, als diese Aufnahme der 1'E Nr. 56.159 mit dem GmP von Erzurum nach Kars im März 1986 entstand.

A stormy sky presaged more snow for the highlands near Soğanlı when this photograph of 2-10-0 no. 56.159 on the daily Erzurum – Kars mixed was taken in March 1986.

RS

Jordanien

Die Überreste der Hedschas-Bahn (Spurweite 1050 mm) bilden das Rückgrat von Jordaniens Eisenbahnnetz. Heute sind die wenigen Züge alle verdieselt, man hält jedoch für Sonderfahrten eine Anzahl von ölgefeuerten Dampflokomotiven in betriebsfähigem Zustand. Da Wasserknappheit und die schlechte Qualität desselben Wüsteneisenbahnen zu frühen Zielen der weltweiten Verdieselung machten, gibt es heute nur noch wenige dampfbetriebene Strecken in Wüstenlandschaften. Die Aufnahme der Pazifiklok Nr. 82 vor einem Sonderzug von Amman nach Katrana entstand im Mai 1983 bei Giza und vermittelt echte Wüstenatmosphäre.

Jordan

The remains of the 1050 mm gauge Hedjaz Railway still forms the backbone of Jordan's railway system. The mostly sparse train service is now normally diesel hauled, but the few remaining serviceable steam locomotives, all oil-fired, see occasional use on special workings. In this photograph, which captures the essence of steam operations in the desert, 4-6-2 no. 82 on a special train between Amman and Katrana is seen near Giza in May 1983. Unfortunately the scarcity and poor quality of water in desert regions made the railways in such areas early targets for dieselization, so that today there are world-wide only a few steam operated desert lines.

ICF

Im Oktober 1985 bewältigt ein Sonderzug nach Katrana, gezogen von der Pazifiklok Nr. 82, die starke Steigung, die durch die Vororte Ammans nach Süden führt. Die Lok gehört zu einem Baulos von 5 Maschinen, die 1953 von Nippon für Thailand gebaut worden waren, aber stattdessen 1959 nach Jordanien geliefert wurden.

In October 1985 a special train to Katrana makes the steep southbound climb through the suburbs of Amman. The locomotive is 4-6-2 no. 82, one of a class of 5 Pacifics built by Nippon in 1953 for Thailand but delivered instead to Jordan in 1959.

HM

Die 1'D1' Nr. 71 (Haine S. Pierre, 1955) verabschiedet sich mit einer Rauchfahne vom Stadtrand von Amman, als sie mit ihrem Sonderzug nach Al Mafraq im September 1985 über eine stilvolle Steinbrücke fährt.

2-8-2 no. 71 (Haine S. Pierre 1955) smokes heavily as it hauls an Amman – Katrana special across an elegant stone viaduct on the outskirts of Amman, September 1985.

HM

Syrien

Syriens Bahnnetz besteht aus Strecken in Normalspur als auch in 1050 mm Spur. Diese ungewöhnliche Spur verdankt ihre Entstehung der Tatsache, daß Eisenschwellen für eine von Damaskus aus geplante meterspurige Strecke mit einem falschen Bohrlochabstand versehen wurden. Um Durchgangsverkehr zu ermöglichen, wurden 1050 mm zu einer Art „Normalspur" für die untereinander verbundenen Strecken in Syrien, im Libanon und in Jordanien, einschließlich der 1300 km langen Hedschas-Bahn von Amman nach Medina. Eine dieser Strecken war die von Damaskus nach Beirut, die die Höhendifferenz vom Mittelmeer ins Libanongebirge mit Hilfe eines 32 km langen Zahnstangenabschnittes bewältigte. Heute wird nur noch der syrische Teil bis Serghaya an der libanesischen Grenze betrieben. Die Aufnahme vom September 1988 zeigt die ölgefeuerte 1'C Tenderlok Nr. 754 (SLM 1894) mit einem Sonderzug von Serghaya nach Damaskus in der Deir Kanum Schlucht.

Syria

The railways in Syria consist of standard and 1050 mm gauge lines. The unusual latter gauge apparently came into being when iron sleepers for a planned metre gauge line from Damascus were drilled to the wrong pitch. To facilitate through traffic 1050 mm then became a common local gauge for interconnecting railways in Syria, Lebanon and Jordan, including the Hedjaz Railway which extended some 1300 km from Damascus to Medina. One line built to this gauge was the Damascus – Beirut Railway, which included a 32 km long rack section for the spectacular ascent into the Lebanese mountains from the Mediterranean coast. Sadly this section is no longer in operation due to the prolonged turmoil in the area, and the Syrian part now functions as a branch terminating at Serghaya on the border with Lebanon. In this September 1988 photograph, oil-fired 2-6-0T no. 754 (SLM 1894), one of the handful of serviceable steam locomotives remaining in Syria, heads through the Deir Kanum gorge with a special train returning to Damascus from Serghaya.

HM

Pakistan

Nach der Teilung des Subkontinents und der Unabhängigkeit von Indien im Jahre 1947 folgte die Traktionspolitik der Pakistanischen Staatsbahn (PR) einem völlig anderen Kurs als die der Indischen Staatsbahn (IR). Während letztere in großem Stil Dampfloks neu bauen ließ, investierte die PR kaum in neue Dampflokomotiven. Dabei gab den Ausschlag, daß nach der Teilung die Kohlevorräte auf indischem Territorium verblieben, und eine stetige Lieferung nicht garantiert war. Deshalb wurden die Dampfloks auf Ölfeuerung umgebaut und nach und nach Diesellokomotiven angeschafft, die bis 1980 alle wichtigen Dienste übernahmen. Zur Freude der Eisenbahnfreunde blieben jedoch viele ältere Baureihen länger in aktivem Einsatz als in Indien.

Die jüngste Breitspurbaureihe war die während und nach dem 2. Weltkrieg angelieferte AWD/CWD 1'D1', von der 96 Stück in den Bestand übernommen wurden. Die ersten BESA (British Engineering Standards Association) Typen, die Güterzug C-Kuppler und die Personenzug 2'B mit Innenzylindern mit der Reihenbezeichnung SGS bzw. SPS (bei Heißdampfausführung) – in Indien kurz nach der Jahrhundertwende eingeführt – zogen bis vor kurzem viele der untergeordneten Züge. Eine andere BESA-Type, die 1'D Reihe HGS aus dem Jahre 1906, war ebenfalls bis in die 80er Jahre im Einsatz, ebenso wie die leichte XA Pazifik, ein IR Standard Design aus den 20er Jahren. All diese Loks sind klassische Vertreter britischer Lokomotivtechnik der entsprechenden Ära.

Die bekannteste pakistanische Eisenbahnlinie war die 52 km lange Strecke auf den Khyber-Paß. Gebaut hauptsächlich für den Truppentransport an die sensible NW-Grenze Britisch-Indiens, erfolgte der Anstieg durch das unwegsame Terrain zum Teil mit Hilfe von Spitzkehren. Noch heute erinnern Festungsanlagen zum Schutz der Brücken an ihre frühere strategische Bedeutung. In den Jahren vor der Stillegung Anfang der 80er Jahre, einer bedauerlichen Auswirkung des Afghanistan-Krieges, bestand das Zugangebot aus einem einmal wöchentlichen GmP von Peshawar nach Landi Kotal, vorne und hinten mit einer SGS bespannt. Eine andere begeisternde Strecke führt von Sibi über den 1800 m hohen Bolan-Paß nach Quetta und Chaman an der afghanischen Grenze. Zur Bewältigung der Steigung waren vor manchen Zügen bis zu vier HGS, je zwei vorne und zwei hinten, erforderlich. Nach der Verdieselung der Strecke versahen die HGS leichtere Aufgaben im Raum Quetta.

Der Einsatz der britischen Oldtimer vor zum Teil herrlicher Gebirgskulisse machten die PR in den Augen der Enthusiasten einzigartig. Wir hoffen, mit den nachfolgenden Bildern einen Eindruck davon zu vermitteln.

Pakistan

After partition from India and independence in 1947 the Pakistan Railways (PR) pursued a very different locomotive policy from that of the Indian Railways. Whereas the latter embarked on a large – scale steam locomotive construction programme, the PR made little investment in new steam traction. A major factor influencing this policy was that after partition the sources of locomotive coal came under Indian control and the supply could not be guaranteed. The existing steam fleet was therefore converted to oil firing and diesels were steadily introduced so that by 1980 none of the most important services was steam worked. For the enthusiast the consequences of this were not entirely negative, as it resulted in older types remaining in active service for longer in Pakistan than in India.

The newest broad gauge class was the AWD/CWD 2-8-2 supplied during and after WW II, of which 96 went into PR stock. However the first British Engineering Standards Association (BESA) designs for India introduced in the early 1900's, the freight 0-6-0 and passenger 4-4-0, both inside – cylindered and classed SGS and SPS respectively when superheated, remained in charge of many lesser services until recent times: some are still in use. Another BESA type, the HGS freight 2-8-0 originally designed in 1906, was also active during the 1980's, as was the XA light 4-6-2, one of the Indian Railway Standard designs of the 1920's. These locomotives, especially the BESA ones, were typical of British practice for the respective periods when they were designed, and the traveller to Pakistan has therefore been able to see in operation locomotives similar to those which were commonplace during the steam era in Britain.

To the enthusiast the best-known of Pakistan's railways is the 52 km long Khyber Pass line from Peshawar to Landi Kotal. Built primarily for the transport of troops to the sensitive NW frontier of British India, it includes reversing stations on its climb through rugged terrain, the fortifications guarding bridges en route being a reminder of its former strategic importance. In latter years its service consisted of a weekly return mixed train, invariably powered by an SGS 0-6-0 at each end of the train. Unfortunately due to repercussions from the recent Afghanistan war the line was closed to traffic in the early 1980's. Another spectacular line leads from Sibi over the 1800 metre high Bolan Pass to Quetta and Chaman. Such is the severity of the Bolan Pass ascent (including 26 km at 4%) that during steam times some trains required four HGS 2-8-0's, two at each end. After being displaced from the Bolan Pass by diesels the HGS's remained at work on the easier stretch of line beyond Quetta.

This combination of Edwardian British locomotives working in sometimes desolate desert-mountain scenery made the PR a unique attraction for the enthusiast, which it is hoped the following pictures will convey.

42

Die öden Berge bei Bostan sind wolkenverhangen, als der tägliche GmP von Quetta nach Chaman dort im Dezember 1980 mit seiner HGS 1'D abfährt.

GH

As storm clouds roll across the desert mountains an HGS 2-8-0 pulls out of Bostan Junction during December 1980 with the daily mixed train from Quetta to Chaman.

Die 1'D HGS 2224 müht sich im März 1983 mit dem 7.00h GmP von Chaman nach Quetta während des langen Anstiegs auf die Khwaja Amran Berge vor der 1950 m hohen Paßhöhe im Khojak Tunnel ab.

HGS 2-8-0 no. 2224 on the 07.00 from Chaman to Quetta toils up the long climb through the Khwaja Amran mountains to the 1950 metre high summit in the Khojak tunnel, March 1983.

DB

Die Strecke von Chaman an der afghanischen Grenze über den Khojak-Paß nach Quetta führt teilweise durch unwirtlichste Ödnis, wie diese Aufnahme einer HGS bei Bostan vor einem in Richtung Quetta eilenden GmP dokumentiert, Dezember 1980.

GH

The sound and movement of a Chaman – Quetta train intrude on the silence and stillness in a scene of absolute desolation near Bostan Junction. The HGS 2-8-0 at the head end in this December 1980 photograph seems to be in a hurry to reach more hospitable territory.

Die 296 km lange Schmalspurbahn (Spurweite 762 mm) von Bostan Junction nach Zhob (ehemals Fort Sandeman) verläuft in nordöstlicher Richtung gro-ßenteils durch wildes Stammesland. Zu sehen ist der wöchentliche GmP nach Zhob, als er bei Toraghbargi den Scheitelpunkt der Strecke in 2222 m Höhe bei Kan Mehtarzai erklimmt. Zuglok ist die 1'D1' Reihe GS Nr. 62, während am Zugschluß eine Baureihe G 1'D1' assistiert, März 1983.

The 296 km long 762 mm gauge line heading northeastwards from Bostan Junction to Zhob (formerly Fort Sandeman) runs for much of its length through wild tribal territories. Here the weekly mixed train to Zhob is seen near Toragh-bargi climbing to the line's summit at Kan Mehtarzai, 2222 metres above sea level, during March 1983. The train is headed by GS class 2-8-2 no. 62 and banked by a G class 2-8-2.

DB

GO

Oben: *Die beiden C-Kuppler SGS Nr. 2471 und 2487 befördern den nur freitags verkehrenden GmP von Peshawar nach Landi Kotal über eine bewachte Brücke zwischen Fort Jamrud und Shahgai. Noch liegt der größte Teil des Anstieges auf den Khyber-Paß vor dem Zug, Januar 1982.*

Links: *Die klassische Aufnahme vom Khyber-Paß: Senkrecht steigen die Rauchsäulen zweier SGS C-Kuppler im Januar 1981 vor dem nur freitags verkehrenden Zug in den Himmel, als dieser der Paßhöhe entgegenfährt. Im Hintergrund sieht man eine Bremsstrecke für bergabrollende Züge.*

Above: *SGS class 0-6-0's nos. 2471 and 2487 take the F.O. Peshawar – Landi Kotal mixed across a guarded bridge between Fort Jamrud and Shahgai near the foot of the main ascent up the Khyber Pass, January 1982.*

Left: *The classic Khyber Pass scene: with SGS 0-6-0's at front and rear sending columns of oil smoke skywards, the F.O. Peshawar – Landi Kotal mixed heads into the mountains during January 1981. Note the escape line for runaway downhill trains in the left background.*

Der gleiche Zug wie auf Seite 46 fährt in einen der kurzen Tunnel der Strecke ein.

GH

The train shown on page 46 is seen here about to enter one of the many short tunnels on the Khyber Pass line.

Hoch türmen sich die Felsen nahe der Paßhöhe des Khyber-Passes, dem sich der GmP von Peshawar nach Landi Kotal im Januar 1981 nähert.

Running under jagged rock formations, the SGS – powered F.O. Peshawar – Landi Kotal mixed train nears the summit of the Khyber Pass, January 1981.

GH

Nicht viel zu tun gibt es für den Oldtimer SGS 2399 in Attock City, Januar 1981.

GH

Portrait of an old-timer: SGS 2399 simmers at Attock City, January 1981.

Frühmorgens im Januar 1981 zieht eine CWD 1'D1' ihren Personenzug in westlicher Richtung aus dem Hauptbahnhof von Rawalpindi.

A CWD 2-8-2 heads out of Rawalpindi station with an early morning westbound passenger train during January 1981.

KO

Bestens gepflegt sind die beiden SGS 2465 und 2467 vor ihrem Zug von Rawalpindi nach Kohat, aufgenommen in der Steigung aus dem Industal zu den Vorbergen des Hindukusch, Januar 1988.

HB

Well – kept SGS 0-6-0's nos. 2465 and 2467 doublehead a Rawalpindi – Kohat train near Babari Banda on the climb from the Indus valley towards the foothills of the Hindu Kush, January 1988.

Der Personenzug L 399 von Wazirabad nach Sialkot und seine Zuglok SPS 2970 werden bei der Ausfahrt aus Sohawala durch die Abendsonne vergoldet, Januar 1979.

The 16.05 train from Wazirabad to Sialkot hauled by SPS 4-4-0 no. 2970 is coloured golden by the setting sun as it heads away from Sohawala, January 1979.

BRC

Malakwal wurde zur letzten Einsatzstelle für die 2'B Maschinen der Baureihe SPS. Zu sehen ist die SPS 3165 bei einer photogenen Ausfahrt mit dem Personenzug 202 nach Khanewal im Januar 1979.

BRC

Malakwal became the last depot to operate the SPS class 4-4-0's. In this view SPS 3165 makes a photogenic departure from Malakwal station with train no. 202, the 06.30 from Lala Musa to Khanewal, in January 1979.

Der Qualm der SGS 4007 in Charali, vor einem langen Güterzug nach Süden, kann sich sehen lassen, während sie an der SPS 2971 vor dem 9.15h Personenzug von Lyallpur nach Lala Musa vorüberfährt. Das Treffen dieser beiden altertümlich wirkenden Lokveteranen, mit einem um die Jahrhundertwende entwickelten, gut durchkonstruierten Design, fand im Januar 1976 statt.

A meeting between the classic turn of the century BESA designs. SGS 0-6-0 no. 4007 hauling a southbound freight smokes heavily as it passes SPS 4-4-0 no. 2971 on the 09.15 Lyallpur – Lala Musa passenger train at Charali in January 1976. Despite the old-fashioned appearance of these locomotives, their design fundamentals were sound.

RM

BRC

Oben: *SPS 3002 verläßt unter einer gewaltigen Qualmwolke den Bahnhof Malakwal mit dem 13.50h Personenzug Lala Musa – Shorkot, März 1983.*

Links: *Die farbenprächtige SGS 2470 meistert die Steigung durch die Salt Range Hills, als sie sich mit dem täglichen Personenzug von Malakwal im Januar 1988 der Endstation Dandot, an der Nebenstrecke von Chalisa Junction gelegen, nähert. (Foto HB).*

Above: *SPS 3002 produces dense black smoke as it leaves Malakwal with the 13.50 Lala Musa – Shorkot train during March 1983.*

Left: *Multicoloured SGS class 0-6-0 no. 2470 climbs through the Salt Range Hills as it nears the terminal station of Dandot on the branch line from Chalisa Junction with the daily train from Malakwal, January 1988. (Photograph HB).*

In Changa Manga, etwa 70 km südlich von Lahore an der elektrifizierten Hauptstrecke nach Khanewal Junction, werden von einer Forstplantage einige kleine holzgefeuerte Tenderloks auf 610 mm Spur eingesetzt. In dieser Szene aus dem November 1983 bahnen sich die Sonnenstrahlen gerade einen Weg durch die Bäume in Changa Manga, während ein Andrew Barclay B-Kuppler umherrangiert, und der Abdampf aus den Zylinderhähnen in der unbewegten, feuchten Luft hängenbleibt. Nach Wassernehmen und Beladen mit Brennholz wird die Lok in den Wald dampfen, um einen mit Holzstämmen beladenen Zug abzuholen.

At Changa Manga, some 70 km south of Lahore on the electrified mainline to Khanewal Junction, there is a forestry plantation served by a 610 mm gauge railway system operating a few small wood-fired tank locomotives. In this November 1983 view, the early morning sunlight is just beginning to filter through the trees at Changa Manga yard as an Andrew Barclay-built 0-4-OWT potters around, the hissing steam from its cylinder drains hanging in the still humid air. After taking on water and wood fuel, the locomotive will head into the forest to collect a loaded log train.

KRC

Indien

Unter den Dampflokomotiven der Indischen Eisenbahnen (IR) dominieren vier Baureihen, die während des intensiven Neubauprogramms der 50er Jahre und der 60er Jahre in großer Stückzahl produziert wurden. Diese sind die WP 2'C1' (755 Stück, gebaut von 1947 bis 1967) und die WG 1'D1' (2450 Stück, 1950–1970) für die 1676 mm Breitspur, sowie die YP 2'C1' (871 Stück, 1949–1970) und die YG 1'D1' (1074 Stück, 1949–1972) für die Meterspur. Diese 5150 Lokomotiven machen ca. 90 % aller nach der Unabhängigkeit 1947 von den IR in Dienst gestellten Dampfloks aus. Von den anderen sind die zahlenmäßig wichtigsten die zwischen 1952 und 1957 gebauten YL 1'C1' für meterspurige Nebenstrecken (264 Stück) und die zwischen 1955 und 1968 gebauten WL Pazifiks für die Breitspur (104 Stück). Hinzu kamen umfangreiche Lieferungen von 1'D1' Universallokomotiven nordamerikanischer sowie kanadischer Hersteller während und nach dem 2. Weltkrieg, AWD/CWD für Breitspur und WD für Meterspur. Diese standen in einer Zahl von 713 bzw. 304 Maschinen auf indischen Gleisen im Einsatz. Ihr Erfolg übte einen starken Einfluß auf das Design der späteren Standardloks aus.

Auch auf der 762 mm Schmalspur wurden zwei aus dem Jahre 1928 stammende Typen (ZB 1'C1' sowie ZE 1'D1') als Standardlokomotiven ausgewählt und in einer Zahl von 43 bzw. 61 Exemplaren, überwiegend in den 50er Jahren, gebaut. Trotz allem erreichte die Standardisierung auf der Schmalspur nicht den gleichen hohen Stand.

Größte Einfachheit ist bezeichnend für die jüngeren indischen Dampfloks. Die einzige ins Auge fallende Ausnahme bei den Standardbaureihen ist die stromlinienförmige Verkleidung der auf der Kesseloberseite liegenden Armaturen bei der Baureihe WP. Diese Schlichtheit rührt her von den Wartungsproblemen, die in einigen Landesteilen existieren, treffend charakterisiert durch den Vorstand eines großen Bahnbetriebswerkes gegenüber einer Besuchergruppe: „Wir haben seit der Unabhängigkeit die Akten in Schuß gehalten, nicht aber die Lokomotiven." Auch die Betriebsabwicklung ist oft lasch, so daß mehrstündige Verspätungen bei Reisezügen an der Tagesordnung sind. Dies trifft aber nicht auf alle Regionen zu. Auf der Meterspur der Western Railway beispielsweise kann man gepflegte und technisch einwandfreie Maschinen vor pünktlichen Zügen erleben.

Gute Landschaftsaufnahmen von indischen Dampfzügen sind nicht leicht zu machen. Die Bedienung von Flachlandstrecken und mäßige Anhängelasten haben meist wenig spektakuläre Einsätze zur Folge. Gewaltige Rauchpilze sind selten und selbst ein früher Wintermorgen garantiert nicht unbedingt eine photogene Dampffahne. Außerdem hüllen sich die Maschinen häufig in ihre eigenen Abdampfwolken ein, sobald der Regler geöffnet wird. Die folgenden Aufnahmen sind somit bei besonders günstigen Gelegenheiten entstanden.

India

Today the Indian Railways (IR) steam scene is dominated by four classes produced in large numbers during the massive locomotive building programme of the late 1940's to early 1970's. These are the WP 4-6-2 (755 locomotives, built 1947–1967) and WG 2-8-2 (2450 locomotives, 1950–1970) on the 1676 mm broad gauge lines, and the YP 4-6-2 (871 locomotives, 1949–1970) and YG 2-8-2 (1074 locomotives, 1949–1972) on the metre gauge lines. These 5150 locomotives represent approximately 90 % of all new steam locomotives put into service by the IR after India became independent in 1947. Of the others, the most important numerically are the 264 YL class 2-6-2's (built 1952–1957) for metre gauge branch lines and the 104 broad gauge WL class 4-6-2's (1955–1968). In addition a large quantity of 2-8-2 mixed traffic locomotives was supplied by American and Canadian manufacturers during and after the 1939–45 war. These are classified AWD/CWD on the broad gauge and WD on the metre gauge and respectively totalled 713 and 304 locomotives operating on IR tracks. The success of certain features of these locomotives had an important influence on the design of the subsequent standard types.

Even on the 762 mm gauge lines two types, both originating in 1928, the ZB 2-6-2 and ZE 2-8-2, were selected as standard designs and eventually totalled 43 and 61 locomotives respectively, mostly constructed in the 1950's. Despite this, standardization on the n.g. lines was never as complete as on the larger gauges.

Utmost simplicity is a key feature of latterday Indian steam locomotives, the only obvious frill on any of the standard classes being the semi-streamlined casing of the WP's. Simplicity is dictated by the maintenance difficulties which clearly exist in certain parts of the country. The situation is aptly summed up by the remark made to a group of visitors by a senior official in the locomotive department that "we have maintained the books, but not the locomotives, since independence". Operating procedures can be similarly lax, and trains running several hours late are not uncommon. However this is not true of all areas. On the Western Railway metre gauge lines for example, clean and well-maintained locomotives can be seen keeping their trains exactly to schedule.

Good photography of Indian steam is not easy. Most steam concentrations are in rather flat and unscenic areas: flat lines and moderate loads result in generally unspectacular operations. Indian locomotives seldom make much smoke, and even winter mornings are not always cold enough for photogenic exhaust trails. Also, when the throttle is opened, the locomotives frequently disappear behind their own leaking steam. The following pictures (grouped according to the regional railway systems of the IR) therefore record scenes where the circumstances influencing photography were more favourable than usual.

Northern Railway: *Geier beäugen im Morgennebel von Khatauli die WP 7105, die mit ihrem Personenzug nach Saharanpur um 4.55h in Meerut City abgefahren ist, Dezember 1983.*

Northern Railway. *Vultures peer through the early morning mist at a WP 4-6-2 standing in Khatauli station with the 04.55 Meerut City – Saharanpur slow passenger train, December 1983.*

DB

Die WP eines Varanasi – Dehra Dun „Janata" Expreßzuges gleißt bei ihrer Abfahrt aus Moradabad im Januar 1984 im Rot der aufgehenden Sonne.

The Varanasi – Dehra Dun "Janata" Express departing from Moradabad behind a WP 4-6-2 is caught by the first golden rays of the rising sun, January 1984.

DW

Die ziemlich schmuddelige WP 7615 zieht im Februar 1980 einen Personenzug durch die westliche Bahnhofsausfahrt von Varanasi.

DB

A rather shabby WP no. 7615 passes some track workers as it starts a westbound passenger train out of Varanasi station during February 1980.

Nur wenige Nahverkehrszüge fahren zwischen den zwei am Ganges liegenden, heiligen Städten Haridwar und Rishikesh. Der Fluß strömt dort aus den Himalayavorbergen in die weite, im Süden liegende Ebene hinaus. Hier überquert im Januar 1984 eine CWD 1'D1' mit dem 8.35h Personenzug von Haridwar nach Rishikesh bei Motichur den ausgetrockneten Lauf eines Gangesarmes.

A sparse service of local trains connects the two holy towns of Haridwar and Rishikesh, both situated on the Ganges where the foothills of the Himalaya mountains rise from the vast plain to the south. Here, a CWD 2-8-2 heading upgrade near Motichur with the 08.35 Haridwar – Rishikesh train crosses the dry riverbed of a tributary of the Ganges, January 1984.

IMW

64

DW

Eine WP hüllt sich im frühen Morgenlicht des Januar 1984 bei ihrer Abfahrt aus Moradabad in Dampf und Rauchwolken ein.

A WP 4-6-2 departing on a westbound express erupts from Moradabad at dawn, January 1984.

Qualm im Übermaß produziert die meterspurige YP 2551 im Februar 1984 vor dem 8.35h Personenzug nach Rewari bei der Ausfahrt aus Jodhpur.

Metre gauge YP 4-6-2 no. 2551 smokes out Jodhpur as it departs on the 08.35 stopping train to Rewari in February 1984.

DW

DW

Einmal wöchentlich im indischen Winter macht der Touristen-Luxuszug „Palast auf Rädern" von Delhi aus eine sechstägige Rundfahrt über die Meterspurstrecken Rajasthans. Der Zug besteht aus den verschwenderisch eingerichteten ehemaligen Salonwagen der früheren Landesfürsten der Staaten Rajasthans. Dieselloks ziehen ihn hauptsächlich. Einer der Abschnitte mit Dampftraktion am Jahresanfang 1984 war von Pokaran nach Jaisalmer. Die Aufnahme entstand in der Wüste Tharr 42 km vor Jaisalmer bei Jetha Chandan, wo die Loks Wasser genommen hatten. Augenscheinlich überläßt die herausgeputzte Zuglok den Löwenanteil der Arbeit ihrer Schwestermaschine am Zugschluß.

Every week during the Indian winter the aptly – named "Palace On Wheels" luxury tourist train departs from Delhi on its six-day round trip over the metre gauge lines of Rajasthan. The train is mostly comprised of lavishly furnished former private coaches of the erstwhile rulers of Rajasthan's Princely States, and is now diesel hauled for most of its journey. Pokaran to Jaisalmer remained one of the few steam hauled sections during early 1984 when the train was photographed leaving the water stop at Jetha Chandan in the Thar wilderness 42 km from Jaisalmer. Of the two YG 2-8-2's powering the train, the banker seems to be doing rather more work than its decorated counterpart at the head end.

Eine Nebenstrecke führt über 295 Kilometer von Jodhpur zur mittelalter-lichen Festungsstadt Jaisalmer in der Wüste Tharr. In dieser Aufnahme aus dem Februar 1984 sind die Stadtmauern stumme Zeugen einer Pazifiklok, die mit dem 8.50h Personenzug nach Jodhpur ausfährt.

The medieval fortress-city of Jaisalmer in the Thar Desert lies at the end of a 295 km long metre gauge branch from Jodhpur. In this February 1984 view, the city walls look down on a YP 4-6-2 departing on the 08.50 passenger train to Jodhpur.

DW

DB

Western Railway: Die Züge 9.40h Mahesana – Kheralu und 6.20h Ahmadabad – Patan liefern sich im Februar 1980 ein Wettrennen bei der Ausfahrt aus Mahesana. Der Zug nach Kheralu (vorne) wird gezogen von der IRS YB Pazifik 30012 (ex Bombay, Baroda & Central India Railway), der Zug nach Patan von der B1 2'C Nr. 31025 (ex Gaekwar's Baroda State Rly.). Beide Maschinen stammen aus dem Jahr 1935.

Western Railway: The 09.40 Mahesana – Kheralu and 06.20 Ahmadabad – Patan trains race each other on the parallel tracks out of Mahesana station during February 1980. The Kheralu train (in the foreground) is headed by IRS YB class 4-6-2 no. 30012 (ex-Bombay Baroda & Central India Rly.) and the Patan train by B1 class 4-6-0 no. 31025 (ex-Gaekwar's Baroda State Rly.): both locomotives date from 1935.

Eine Licht/Schatten Studie, aufgenommen im Bahnhof Agra Fort im Januar 1986. Die markante Front einer WP hebt sich klar von dem dampf- und lichterfüllten Hintergrund ab. Ein genauer Blick auf einige der Lokomotivdetails enthüllt den traurigen Zustand, in dem viele der indischen Dampflokomotiven heute ihren Dienst tun.

In this study of light and shade taken inside Agra Fort station during January 1986, the distinctive frontal features of a WP contrast with the transient form of the steam rising in the background. Some of the locomotive's details display the rather sad condition in which much of Indian Railways steam now operates.

GH

Der letzte durchgehend dampfgeführte Schnellzug auf der Meterspur südwest-lich von Delhi war der Delhi mit Udaipur verbindende „Chetak-Expreß". Nahe seinem südlichen Ziel durchquert der Zug mit seiner YP im Februar 1984 die wilde Landschaft Rajasthans bei Debari. Laut Aussage eines lokalen Bahn-hofsvorstandes sollen in dieser Gegend Leoparden und Tiger (diese weniger häufig) ihr Unwesen treiben und ihren Speiseplan gelegentlich mit ahnungs-losen Eisenbahnfreunden aufbessern.

DW

In this February 1984 photograph taken near Debari the Delhi – Udaipur "Che-tak Express" hauled by a YP 4-6-2 is seen running through a wild Rajasthan landscape which hints at the mystery of India and where, according to a local stationmaster, leopards and (more improbably) tigers were still roaming, ready to devour unsuspecting railfans.

Unter der eindrucksvollen Signalbrücke an der südlichen Bahnhofsausfahrt von Ajmer fährt im Februar 1984 die YP 2301 mit dem 9.00h Zug nach Kacheguda durch.

Class YP no. 2301 making a vigorous start with the 09.00 train to Kacheguda passes under the impressive signal gantry to the south of Ajmer station, February 1984.

IMW

Die abendliche Silhouette der C1' Baureihe W Nr. 585 kommt vor dem 16.15h Zug von Bhavnagar nach Mahuva auf der 762 mm-Spur Strecke bei Bhadi voll zur Geltung, Februar 1980.

DB

W class 0-6-2 no. 585 heads into the sunset with the 16.15 Bhavnagar – Mahuva train on the 762 mm gauge line linking these two towns: photographed near Bhadi during February 1980.

Wie ein einäugiges, rauchspeiendes Ungeheuer, einge-
hüllt in Dampfwolken, stürmt eine WP mit ihrer bulligen
Rundnase auf den Fotografen zu, als sie im Januar 1986
aus Agra Fort ausfährt.

An enveloping steam cloud clears to reveal the bulbous
front of a WP bearing down on the photographer like a
one-eyed smoke-throwing monster as it blasts out of
Agra Fort station during January 1986.

GH

Eine YP der Northern Railway stürmt im Januar 1984 mit dem Marudhar Expreß nach Jodhpur bei der Ausfahrt aus Jaipur an einem Wald aus Signalen vorbei.

IMW

A Northern Railway YP 4-6-2 passes a forest of signals as it storms away from Jaipur (Western Railway) with the "Marudhar Express" to Jodhpur, January 1984.

Central Railway: *Durch ihr markantes Profil ist die Baureihe WP zu einem Symbol des Dampfbetriebes in Indien geworden. Diese Nachtaufnahme aus dem Bw Bhusaval, dem größten Bw der CR Ende der 70er Jahre, gibt im Scheinwerferlicht der WP 7414 die rußerfüllte Depotatmosphäre wieder, Januar 1981.*

Central Railway. *Due to its stylish profile the WP class has become the symbol of Indian steam. In this night scene recorded during January 1981 at Bhusaval, then the CR's largest depot, the smoky shed atmosphere is cut through by the powerful beam from the headlight of WP 7414.*

BRC

Westlich von Dhaulpur verläuft eine Schmalspurbahn in 762 mm Spur. Der 9.15h GmP nach Tantpur verläßt im November 1984 mit der ZA/3 1'D2't Nr. 735 den Ort Bari, ein typisches indisches Dorf. Bei den Kamelen handelt es sich anscheinend nicht um Eisenbahnfreunde.

On the 762 mm gauge line running westwards from Dhaulpur, ZA/3 class 2-8-4T no. 735 heads the 09.15 Dhaulpur – Tantpur mixed train away from Bari, a typically ramshackle Indian village, during November 1984. The camels, it would seem, are not railway enthusiasts.

HB

Der Vollmond steht über der schmalspurigen (762 mm) Lok ZE Nr. 52, die gerade mit dem abendlichen Zug aus Baramati in Daund, an der Hauptstrecke Bombay – Madras gelegen, angekommen ist, Dezember 1981.

The full moon hangs in the sky above 762 mm gauge ZE class 2-8-2 no. 52 which has just arrived at Daund on the Bombay – Madras main line with the evening branch line passenger train from Baramati, December 1981.

RS

Southern Railway. Oben: *Das Beste, was der Dampfbetrieb in Indien zu bieten hatte, ist in dieser Aufnahme aus dem Februar 1980 zu sehen. Eine WP mit dem „Nilagiri-Expreß" nach Madras tobt aus dem Bahnhof von Mettupalaiyam hinaus. (Foto DB).*

Links: *Die 46 km lange Meterspurstrecke von Mettupalaiyam in den Ferienort Ootacamund (Udagamandalam) in den Nilgiribergen ist Indiens einzige Zahnradstrecke. Der Scheitelpunkt liegt bei 2203 m, die Steigung beträgt maximal 40 °/oo auf Adhäsionsabschnitten und 80 °/oo auf Zahnstangenabschnitten. Alle Züge fahren mit den zwölf D1' Tenderlokomotiven der Reihe X, Vierzylinder-Verbundloks, die speziell für diese Strecke zwischen 1914 und 1952 beschafft wurden. Während Nebelschleier über dem bei Ootacamund gelegenen See tanzen, dampft Lok 37389 mit dem 8.00h Zug nach Coonor vorbei, Januar 1987.*

Southern Railway. Above: *The best in Indian steam is pictured in this February 1980 view of a WP powering out of Mettupalaiyam with the Madras-bound "Nilagiri Express". (Photograph DB).*

Left: *The 46 km long metre gauge line from Mettupalaiyam to the resort of Ootacamund in the Nilagiri Hills is India's only rack railway. The highest altitude reached is 2203 metres and the maximum gradients are 4% and 8% on adhesion and rack sections respectively. All traffic is worked by the twelve X class 4-cylinder compound rack and adhesion 0-8-2T's built specially for this line over the period 1914–52. Here steam is rising from the lake outside Ootacamund as loco no. 37389 passes with the 08.00 train to Coonoor during January 1987.*

Ganz anders wirkt dieses Bild wie das auf Seite 78, das ebenfalls im Januar 1987 aufgenommen wurde und den gleichen Zug an fast der gleichen Stelle zeigt, Zuglok ist dieses Mal die X 37387.

GH

This January 1987 photograph of the 08.00 Ootacamund – Coonoor train headed by class X no. 37387, running over an adhesion section shortly after leaving Ootacamund, provides an interesting contrast with the picture on page 78, both having been taken at the same location.

Obwohl die WG 1'D1' die häufigste indische Dampflokbaureihe ist, sind gute Streckenaufnahmen dieser Baureihe ziemlich selten. Die Maschinen sind oft in schlechtem Unterhaltungszustand und ihr Einsatz ist meist auf untergeordnete Dienste beschränkt. Auf diesem Bild verläßt die WG 8969 qualmend Bangalore mit dem 7.45h Zug nach Madras, März 1978.

Despite being the most numerous of all IR locomotives, the WG class 2-8-2's are now mostly used on menial duties and are often poorly maintained; consequently good action photographs of this class are comparatively rare. In this view, WG 8969 makes an exceptionally smoky start from Bangalore with the 07.45 train to Madras, March 1978.

BRC

South Eastern Railway. Oben: *Körperlich sehr anstrengend ist die in vielen indischen Bahnbetriebswerken übliche Bekohlung von Hand. Ein Blick ins Bw Baripada, an der 762 mm Schmalspurbahn Rupsa – Bangriposi, westlich von Kalkutta, zeigt eine ZE 1'D1' beim Bekohlen. Dahinter wartet eine CC Pazifik, Dezember 1985.*

Rechts: *Die SER betreibt auf ihrem 762 mm Netz den größten Teil der Schmalspurdampflokomotiven der Indischen Staatsbahn. In Ranchi, dem Ausgangsbahnhof der Strecke nach Lohardaga, rangierte im Dezember 1985 die ZE 1'D1' Nr. 99, während Einheimische nach der Kühle der Nacht gerade die sanfte Wärme der ersten Sonnenstrahlen genießen.*

Beide GH

South Eastern Railway. Above: *The manual coaling of locomotives, a familiar scene at many Indian depots, is physically very arduous work. In this December 1985 view of Baripada shed on the 762 mm gauge Rupsa – Bangriposi line west of Calcutta, a ZE 2-8-2 is being coaled whilst a CC class 4-6-2 stands in the background.*

Right: *The night is always coldest for those with no home to sleep in, but it is for them that the rising sun shines the brightest. As local people rejoice in the warmth which comes with the passing of night into day, a ZE class 2-8-2 pauses in its shunting duties, as if to join them in paying homage to the sun. Photographed at Ranchi, terminus of the 762 mm gauge line from Lohardaga, during December 1985.*

KRC

Eastern Railway: WP 7143 streckt ihre dekorierte Nase aus einem Torbogen im Bw Jhajha, Oktober 1981.

Eastern Railway: WP 7143 pokes its decorated nose-cone through an archway in Jhajha's depot building, October 1981.

Ein Zug von Patna nach Kalkutta (Howrah), geführt von der WP 7578 und geschoben von einer WG 1'D1', erklimmt die 10 ⁰/₀₀ Steigung auf die Rajmaha Hügel südlich von Jhajha, Dezember 1980.

A Patna – Calcutta (Howrah) train headed by WP 4-6-2 no. 7578 and banked by a WG 2-8-2 climbs the 1% gradient leading to the Rajmaha Hills south of Jhajha, December 1980.

HB

Die unverwechselbare Silhouette einer WP mit einem Personenzug nach Patna hebt sich bei Jehanabad gegen die aufgehende Sonne ab, 1. Januar 1986.

GH

On New Year's Day 1986 the rising sun silhouettes the distinctive profile of a WP 4-6-2 leaving Jehanabad on a Gaya – Patna stopping train.

North Eastern Railway: Indien wie im Bilderbuch: Menschen, Tiere und Transportmittel versammeln sich an einem Wintervormittag im Bahnhof von Suraimanpur, während der von der YP 2501 gezogene Personenzug von Barauni nach Varanasi dort im Januar 1986 hält.

North Eastern Railway. The Indian scene: assorted people, animals and conveyances assemble on a winter's morning at Suraimanpur station to attend the stopover of a Barauni – Varanasi train headed by YP 4-6-2 no. 2501, January 1986.

GH

Ein Gegenzug muß abgewartet werden und die Signale sind rot für eine YP Pazifiklok im Bahnhof Muktapur. In wenigen Minuten wird der Endbahnhof Samastipur erreicht sein, Januar 1986.

As it waits for a crossing at Muktapur station, a YP 4-6-2 on a train for Samastipur faces a row of red signals which bar a passage ahead into the Indian night, January 1986.

GH

Der Meterspurexpreß 24 der NER nach Lucknow mit Abfahrt in Kanpur um 7.30 h bestand üblicherweise aus 21 Wagen und wurde von zwei YP gezogen. Der Zug ist hier im Februar 1984 bei der Ausfahrt aus Kanpur Central zu sehen. In der Mitte und links sind die NR Breitspurstrecken nach Lucknow und Allahabad zu sehen, und im Hintergrund eine Straße, auf der etwas später das übliche Gedränge einsetzen wird.

NER train no. 24, the 07.15 Kanpur – Lucknow metre gauge express, normally totalled 21 coaches hauled by double-headed YP's. This train is seen here snaking out of Kanpur Central in February 1984. At the centre and left are the NR broad gauge tracks to Lucknow and Allahabad respectively, and in the background is a typical Indian urban street, still uncrowded at this early hour.

IMW

Nur zaghaft durchdringt die Sonne Morgennebel und Rauch, eine Fahrradrik-schah schwankt ächzend über die krummen Geleise, sein Fahrer dick ver-mummt gegen die Kälte der Nacht, arme Leute durchstreifen die Bahnanlagen auf der Suche nach Schätzen wie zum Beispiel Kohle, ein Muezzin ruft die Gläubigen von der nahen Moschee durchdringend zum Gebet, und in dieser Alltagsszene erfüllt eine WG ihren Rangierdienst, Muzaffarpur, Januar 1986.

GH

Smog and smoke defying the sunlight; a creaking cycle rickshaw crossing kinked and crooked rails, its driver and passenger wrapped up against the cold; poor people scavenging the trackside for treasures such as coal; the haunting call from a mosque of a muezzin commanding the faithful to pray. Amongst these typical ingredients of the early morning Indian scene, a WG 2-8-2 per-forms its shunting chores at Muzaffarpur station, January 1986.

Northeast Frontier Railway: *Für die meisten Eisenbahnfreunde ist die Darjeeling Himalaya Bahn der NFR (Spurweite 610 mm) die Hauptattraktion Indiens. Auf 87 km Länge klettert die Bahn von fast Meeresniveau bei New Jalpaiguri durch dichte Wälder bis zum 2258 m hohen Scheitelpunkt bei Ghum, von wo aus die Strecke bis Darjeeling wieder fällt. Dort eröffnet sich ein unbeschreiblicher Ausblick auf die Gipfel des Himalaya im Norden. Die maximale Streckensteigung liegt bei 50 ⁰/₀₀, und es gibt sowohl Spitzkehren als auch Schleifen, um an Höhe zu gewinnen. Die B-Kuppler der Reihe B mit Sattel- und Rahmentanks, erstmals 1889 gebaut, haben über 100 Jahre hinweg praktisch den gesamten Verkehr bewältigt. Ihre gedrungene Bauweise ist den engen Kurven angepaßt. Die Maschinchen werden auf den langen Steigungen nach Ghum bis an ihre Grenze beansprucht und von den Werkstätten in Tindharia aus verständlichen Gründen bestens unterhalten. In dieser Aufnahme vom November 1978 ist der dritte Teil des 7.10h Zuges von New Jalpaiguri nach Darjeeling zu sehen. Der Rauch der Lok 779 „Mountaineer" (Sharp Stewart 1892) quillt durch die Bäume auf dem Streckenabschnitt zwischen Yayaban und Mahanadi.*

Northeast Frontier Railway. *For most enthusiasts India's greatest attraction is the 610 mm gauge Darjeeling Himalayan Railway of the NFR. With a route length of 87 km, this line climbs from near sea level at New Jalpaiguri through densely forested hills to the 2258 metre summit at Ghum before descending to Darjeeling, from where there are superb views of the Himalayan peaks to the north. The maximum gradient is 5 % and both reversing stations and loops are used to gain height. The B class 0-4-0 saddle + well tank locomotives first built in 1889 have almost monopolized train workings on the DHR for a hundred years. A compact design because of the railway's tight curves, they are worked at full power on the long climb to Ghum and are of necessity kept in excellent condition by the line's workshops at Tindharia. In this November 1978 view of the third portion of the 07.10 New Jalpaiguri – Darjeeling train, the smoke from hardworking B class no. 779 "Mountaineer" (Sharp Stewart 1892) mingles with the trees overlooking the section of line between Yayaban and Mahanadi.*

DB

DW

Oben: An einem wolkenreichen Februartag 1984 nimmt der 6.40h Zug von Kurseong nach Darjeeling die Steigung bei Ghum. Deutlich zu erkennen sind die für die Darjeeling Himalaya Bahn typischen, extrem engen Kurven.

Links: Der 6.40h Zug von Kurseong nach Darjeeling wird haupt-sächlich von Schülern benutzt. Lok 783 der Reihe B (Sharp Stewart 1899) nähert sich im Februar 1984 der Station Ghum. Einige der jugendlichen Reisenden machen sich einen Spaß daraus, neben dem Zug herzulaufen.

Above: A class B 0-4-0 T on the 06.40 Kurseong – Darjeeling train climbs to Ghum on a cloudy day in February 1984. This view shows the extremely severe curvature which characterises the Darjeeling Himalayan Railway.

Left: The 06.40 train from Kurseong to Darjeeling is run primarily to ferry children to school. Class B no. 783 (Sharp Stewart 1899) approaches Ghum on this service during February 1984, with some of the passengers indulging in the sport of racing their own train.

DB

Industriebahnen: *In Indien gibt es viele Industriebahnen verschiedener Spurweiten, auf denen interessante und zum Teil sehr alte Lokomotiven den Dienst versehen. Hier schlängelt sich die B1't Nr. 19 (Barclay 1917) im Januar 1984 mit einem Züglein durch dichten Wald auf der 762 mm Schmalspurstrecke der Industriebahn der Indian Iron & Steel Co. in Manoharpur, westlich von Jamshedpur.*

Industrial Railways. *India has many industrial railways of various gauges operating interesting and sometimes very old steam locomotives. In this example, 0-4-2 T no. 19 (Barclay 1917) meanders through dense forest with a short train on the Indian Iron & Steel Co.'s 762 mm gauge railway at Manoharpur, west of Jamshedpur, during January 1984.*

Nepal

Die Schmalspurbahn in 762 mm Spur von Jaynagar in Indien nach Bizalpura in Nepal wird sehr stark von Hindupilgern in Anspruch genommen. Die C1' Tender-lok „Chandra" (Hunslet 1962) befördert hier im Februar 1980 bei Khajuri den 16.10 h Personenzug von Jaynagar nach Janakpur Dham. Die Bahnverwaltung sollte mit den Fahrgastzahlen eigentlich zufrieden sein. Es ist jedoch nicht bekannt, wie viele der Reisenden tatsächlich im Besitz einer gültigen Fahrkarte waren.

Nepal

The 762 mm gauge Janakpur Railway from Jaynagar in India to Bizalpura in Nepal carries heavy Hindu pilgrimage traffic. Here 0-6-2 T "Chandra" (Hunslet 1962) heading the 16.10 Jaynagar – Janakpur train is pictured entering Khajuri station in February 1980. The railway's management should be satisfied with the passenger loading, but it is not known how many of those aboard have actually bothered to pay the fare.

DB

GH

Oben: Burma. *Auf Burmas Meterspurnetz verkehren nur noch wenige Dampflokomotiven. In der Endstation Madauk der Nebenstrecke von Pyuntaza (an der Hauptstrecke Rangun – Mandalay) geht auf die schmutzige YP Pazifik und ihren Nahverkehrszug gerade ein heftiger Monsunschauer nieder. Einige Reisende erbringen den Beweis, daß die Lokomotive auch als Packwagen dienen kann, September 1983.*

Rechts: Thailand. *Kurz bevor die meterspurige Thailändische Staatsbahn ihren Dampfbetrieb einstellte, überquert der 6.00h GmP von Bangkok Thonburi nach Nam Tok im November 1975 mit einer holzgefeuerten japanischen C 56 1'C vorsichtig eine wacklig wirkende Holzbrücke bei Wang Pho. Die Strecke gehört zu der aus dem 2. Weltkrieg berüchtigten Burma-Siam-Bahn über den 3-Pagoden-Paß nach Burma, die schon lange stillgelegt ist.*

Above: Burma. *In heavy monsoon rain during September 1983 one of Burma Railway's few remaining steam locomotives, a grimy oil-fired metre gauge YB 4-6-2 (a 1920's Indian Railway Standard Design) stands at the branch line terminus of Madauk with a train to Pyuntaza on the Rangoon – Mandalay line. Amid the sodden bustle some passengers show that the engine can also serve as a baggage car.*

Right: Thailand. *In November 1975, near the end of normal steam workings on the metre gauge Royal State Railway of Thailand, the 06.00 Bangkok Thonburi – Nam Tok mixed behind a log-fired ex-Japanese C56 class 2-6-0 slowly crosses a creaking wooden trestle bridge by the Kwai Noi River near Wang Pho. This line forms part of the infamous WWII – built Burma – Siam railway; the tracks into Burma via Three Pagodas Pass have long been closed.*

HB

Indonesien

Das Streckennetz der Indonesischen Staatsbahn (PJKA) besteht im wesentlichen aus der 1067 mm Spur, die auf Java und Sumatra während der holländischen Kolonialzeit angelegt worden war. Das javanische Netz ist, angemessen für eine der dichtest besiedelten Regionen der Welt, recht ausgedehnt. Im Gegensatz dazu ist Sumatra großenteils von undurchdringlichen, sumpfigen Regenwäldern bedeckt, so daß die Bevölkerungsdichte und der Entwicklungsstand allgemein geringer blieben. Die Eisenbahnstrecken sind aus diesem Grund unzusammenhängend und erschließen nur bestimmte Teile der Insel.

Ein Sammelsurium von Dampflokomotiven wurde erworben, die Höchstzahl von ca. 1200 Maschinen wurde nach dem 2. Weltkrieg erreicht. Leichte Schienen und die, wegen der starken Niederschläge, ständig drohende Gefahr des Absackens des Oberbaus erforderten äußerst niedrige Achslasten. Die höchste betrug 13 Tonnen bei der 1'D1' Baureihe D 52, von der Krupp 1951 100 Stück lieferte. Dies war die größte Anzahl, die von einer einzelnen Baureihe nach Indonesien gelangte und auch die letzte von der PJKA bezogene Mehrzweckmaschine. Auf ebenen Strecken und in untergeordneten Diensten wurden zum Teil sehr kleine Lokomotiven verwendet, z. B. die Reihe B 52, ein B-Kuppler mit einem Gesamtgewicht von 17 Tonnen aus den Jahren 1908–1913. Die geringen Achslasten erforderten auf den Bergstrecken vielfach-gekuppelte Dampflokomotiven. Verschiedene Serien von Verbund- Mallets, sowohl in Tender- als auch in Schlepptenderausführung, wurden beschafft, von denen die größte die 1'D'D der Reihe DD 52 war. Von der bemerkenswerten F10 1'E1' Tenderlok wurden 28 Stück zwischen 1912 und 1920 geliefert. Dies war einer der wenigen produzierten Sechskuppler, und offenbar erfolgreich, wie sein hohes Dienstalter beweist.

Als Brennstoff wurden Kohle, Öl und Holz benutzt. Kohle wird bei Padang in West-Sumatra und bei Tanjungenim in Süd-Sumatra gefördert. Die meisten Lokomotiven in Sumatra waren deshalb kohlegefeuert. Als Indonesien zu einem wichtigen Erdölproduzenten aufstieg, wurde Öl auch zum bevorzugten Brennstoff für die meisten Lokomotiven, zumindest in Java.

Ab den 50er Jahren ging es mit den PJKA Dampflokomotiven langsam bergab, als Folge der Verdieselung und Streckenstillegungen auf Grund des zunehmenden Kraftverkehrs. Mitte der 80er Jahre war der Dampfbetrieb praktisch erloschen. Trotzdem ist Indonesien für den Enthusiasten immer noch interessant wegen der vielen schmalspurigen Zuckerrohrbahnen. Diese besitzen herrliche Sammlungen winziger, oft bunt-lackierter Lokomotiven, die während der Entezeit unermüdlich das Zuckerrohr von den Feldern zu den Fabriken befördern, oder in den Fabriken rangieren.

Die folgenden Bilder von PJKA Lokomotiven auf Java und Sumatra, sowie von einigen Zuckerrohrbahnen, vermitteln einen Einblick in die üppige Tropenvegetation Indonesiens und bilden einen Kontrast zu den meist ariden oder kühleren Gegenden, die sonst in dieser Buchreihe vorherrschen.

Indonesia

The Indonesian State Railways (PJKA) consists basically of the 1067 mm gauge system developed in Java and Sumatra during Dutch colonial rule. The Javan railway network is quite extensive as befits one of the world's most heavily populated regions. By contrast Sumatra is mostly covered by dense and often marshy rain forest resulting in a much lower population density and general level of development. Its railways are therefore isolated lines serving only certain parts of the island.

A diverse steam locomotive fleet was built up reaching a maximum total of about 1200 locomotives after WW II. Light track and the risk of roadbed subsidence due to the area's heavy rainfall dictated extremely low axleloads for all locomotives, the heaviest being the 13 tons of the 100 D 52 2-8-2's delivered by Krupp in 1951. These were the most numerous single class in Indonesia and also the last general-purpose steam locomotives acquired by the PJKA. For flat lines and minor services some very small locomotives were used, e.g. the B 52 class 0-4-0's of 1908–13 with an engine weight of only 17 tons. However the light axleloads necessitated multi-axle locomotives for mountain sections. Several series of compound Mallets were introduced of both tank and tender types, the largest being the DD 52 2-8-8-0's. A notable class was the F10 2-12-2T, 28 of which were delivered during 1912–20. This was one of the very few twelve-coupled designs ever put into service and by virtue of a long active life it appears to have been successful.

Coal, oil and wood firing have all been used on the PJKA. Coal of reasonable quality is mined near Padang in Sumatra, and locomotives based in this area were therefore coal fired. Wood is plentiful and was burnt in some locomotives operating minor services. However Indonesia is a major oil producer and consequently oil became the preferred fuel for most locomotives.

From the 1950's onwards PJKA steam went into gradual decline due to the spread of dieselization and the contraction of railway services as a result of road competition. By the mid 1980's steam workings had effectively ceased. However Indonesia is still attractive for the enthusiast because of the many n.g. railways belonging to sugar plantations. These have fascinating collections of tiny and often brightly painted locomotives which are kept busy during harvest times hauling loads of sugar cane from the fields to the processing factories. Unusually for sugar plantation locomotives they are often oil fired, although bagasse fuel is also used.

The following pictures, showing PJKA operations in Sumatra and Java and a glimpse of the sugar plantation railways, illustrate the lush tropical settings in which Indonesian steam worked and which provide a strong contrast to the mostly arid or cold areas featured elsewhere in this series.

DB

Sumatras interessanteste Bahn liegt nahe dem Äquator und dient überwiegend dem Kohletransport von den Zechen bei Sawahlunto zum Hafen bei Padang. Der Streckenabschnitt bis Padang Panjang weist bis zu 70‰ steile Zahnstangenabschnitte auf. Fünffach gekuppelte Tenderloks mit 4 Zylindern wurden zwischen 1922 und 1928 von Esslingen und SLM für diese Strecke gebaut. Weitere 17 Maschinen wurden zwischen 1964 und 1967 von Esslingen und Nippon Sharyo geliefert. Dies waren die letzten von der Staatsbahn beschafften Dampflokomotiven. Sie erreichten ein nur kurzes Dienstalter, da die Strecken zu Beginn der 80er Jahre verdieselt wurden. Zu sehen ist die E 10 67 mit einem Kohlezug im Zahnstangenabschnitt zwischen Batutabal und Sumpur oberhalb des Singkarak-Sees, 1. 5. 1981.

Sumatra's most interesting railway, for coal transport from mines at Sawahlunto to the port near Padang, lies close to the equator. From Sawahlunto it climbs to Padang Panjang reaching 773 m a.s.l. before descending to Padang, both sections being partly rack with up to 7% grades. The line received 17 4-cylinder compound 0-10-0 rack and adhesion tank locomotives (PJKA class E10) from Esslingen and SLM in 1922–28, and 17 replacement E10's from Esslingen and Nippon Sharyo in 1964–67. Unfortunately dieselization in the early 1980's ended steam workings, although some E10's were kept in reserve. Here, Giesl-fitted E1067 (the last steam locomotive delivered to the PJKA) storms uphill through rain forest on the rack section between Batutabal and Sumpur with a coal train, May 1981.

Zwei E 10 Lokomotiven mit 3 leeren Kohlewagen rollen gemeinsam über den Zahnstangenabschnitt zum Singkarak-See hinab, August 1980. (Foto GH).

Two E10 class locomotives straddling three empty trucks for the mines roll downhill over the rack section above Lake Singkarak in August 1980. (GH)

Die kohlegefeuerte 1'D1' D 52 004 posiert vor einem kleinen Publikum im Bw Tanjungenim in Südsumatra, August 1983.

Coal-fired D52 class 2-8-2 no. 004 poses before a small audience at Tanjungenim depot, August 1983.

GH

Nur ein paar Sonnenstrahlen sorgen für notdürftige Beleuchtung, als sich ein Mechaniker am Dampfdom der D 52 004 im Bw Tanjungenim zu schaffen macht, August 1983.

GH

A few precious rays of sunlight provide the only illumination for the fitter working on the steam turret of D 52004 inside the gloomy interior of Tanjungenim shed during August 1983.

Java: Eine der letzten PJKA Strecken mit Dampfbetrieb war die im äußersten Westen Javas gelegene Nebenstrecke von Rangkasbitung nach Labuan. Normalerweise wurde das tägliche Personenzugpaar von der Baureihe B 51 geführt, einer Zweizylinder-Verbundlok der Achsfolge 2'B, deren Überleben bis in die jüngste Zeit als fast unglaublich anzusehen ist. Auf dem Bild halten sowohl das offizielle als auch das inoffizielle „Personal" der B 51 38 angestrengt Ausschau nach vorne, während sie sich ihrem Ziel Rangkasbitung nähern, Juli 1983.

Java. One of the last steam-worked lines on the PJKA was the branch from Rangkasbitung to Labuan at the western tip of Java. Motive power for the daily round trip was usually a B51 class 2-cylinder compound 4-4-0, a most unlikely type to survive into recent times. In this photograph taken in July 1983, B5138's official and unofficial locomotive crews both keep a sharp lookout ahead as they approach Rangkasbitung with the train from Labuan.

GH

Lok 38, die letzte aktive Vertreterin dieser Baureihe, pausiert an einem Juliabend 1983 in Labuan. Als im Jahr darauf die Lok schließlich aus dem Verkehr gezogen wurde, nahm man dies als Anlaß, auch gleich die ganze Strecke stillzulegen.

KRC

B5138, the last active member of its class, rests at Labuan shed during a July night in 1983. The following year this locomotive finally expired, whereupon the entire line from Rangkasbitung was closed.

Mit 2 heruntergekommenen Wägelchen ist die B 51 38 im Juli 1983 in Richtung Rangkasbitung unterwegs.

Two decrepit and rust-eaten four-wheel coaches forming the train from Labuan head for Rangkasbitung behind B 5138 during July 1983.

GH

Naß vom Regen gleißen die Schienen an der Einfahrt zum Bw Rang-kasbitung, vor dem die BB 10 05 in einer Juninacht 1980 posiert. Diese Mallet-Tenderlok aus dem Jahre 1899 fuhr nur fallweise in Rich-tung Labuan.

Glistening rails lead to the entrance of Rangkasbitung depot where BB1005 stands on a rainy night during June 1980. This 0-4-4-2 Mallet tank of 1899 vintage was a rare performer on the Labuan branch.

KRC

Einige Sonnenstrahlen durchdringen den Dunst in einer kleinen Lichtung im Regenwald West-Javas, den die B 51 38 gerade mit ihrem Personenzug nach Rangkasbitung durchfährt, Juli 1983.

Shafts of light slanting through the humid air illuminate the clearing in the lush West Javan forest through which B5138 is glimpsed heading for Rangkasbitung in July 1983.

KRC

GH

Links: *Die 1'D1' Tenderlok D 14 12 verqualmt die Umgebung auf ihrer Lz-Fahrt von Cianjur nach Padalarang, wohin sie zum Rangieren fährt. Obwohl die ölgefeuerte Lok keine Last zu befördern hatte, mußte sie wegen Dampfmangels auf freier Strecke anhalten, Juli 1983.*

Rechts: *Die 1'C'C Verbundmallets der Reihe CC 50 sind die wohl bekannteste der indonesischen Dampflokbaureihen. Die Portraitaufnahme zeigt die grüne CC 50 19 an einem Augustmorgen 1978 beim Rangieren in Purwakarta.*

Left: *Class D14 2-8-2 T no. 12 fills the air with oil smoke whilst travelling light engine from Cianjur to do some shunting at Padalarang in July 1983. Despite the zero trailing load the locomotive managed to run out of steam during this trip.*

Right: *The CC 50 class 2-6-6-0 compound Mallets became perhaps the best-known of all Indonesian steam classes. In this August 1978 portrait, green-painted CC 5019 performing shunting work at Purwakarta glints in the tropical sunlight.*

Rechts: Die Nebenstrecke Cibatu – Garut – Cikajang war das letzte Einsatzgebiet der CC 50 Mallets. Hier zieht die CC 50 12 ihren Personenzug von Cibatu nach Cikajang mit voller Kraft über die Steigung zwischen Garut und Bayongbong, August 1980.

Links: Etwas zu groß geraten für ihren Zwei-Wagen-Zug scheint die CC 50 Mallet, die gerade mit dem 12.50 h Zug von Cibatu nach Cikajang den Fluß Cimanuk in Garut überquert, Dezember 1980.

Right: The Cibatu – Garut – Cikajang branch was the last line operated by the CC 50 2-6-6-0 Mallets. Here, CC 5012 at the head of the 12.50 Cibatu – Cikajang train is seen storming upgrade between Garut and Bayongbong during August 1980.

Left: Seemingly an outsize locomotive for hauling two coaches, a CC 50 class Mallet hurries the 12.50 Cibatu – Cikajang train over the River Cimanuk at Garut during December 1980.

GH

GH

Oben: *Über der Bahnhofshalle von Cibatu erhebt sich in der Ferne der dunstige Umriß des 2249 m hohen Vulkans Guntur. Reisende warten auf einen Expreß nach Bandung, andere sind im Begriff, in den Personenzug nach Garut mit seiner CC 50 03 einzusteigen, August 1983.*

Links: *Im August 1978 überquert die CC 50 24 in luftiger Höhe eine hohe Brücke bei Bayongbong mit einem Personenzug von Cibatu nach Cikajang. Den Passagieren auf dem Tender eröffnet sich ein ungehinderter Rundblick auf die prachtvolle Landschaft, durch die diese Nebenstrecke führt.*

Above: *The hazy outline of the 2249 metre volcano Mt. Guntur stands high above the overall-roofed station at Cibatu where passengers are assembling for a branch line train towards Garut hauled by CC 5003, August 1983.*

Left: *CC 5024 looks a fine sight as it crosses a bridge above Bayongbong with the morning Cibatu – Cikajang train in August 1978. Some of the passengers appear to find the tender the best place from which to view the beautiful tropical scenery found on this line.*

Links: *Der inzwischen stillgelegte Abschnitt von Garut nach Cikajang wies Steigungen bis 40 ⁰/₀₀ auf, was für die Mallets trotz der kurzen Züge Schwerarbeit bedeutete. Zu sehen ist eine CC 10 Mallet-Tenderlok der Achsfolge 1'C'C auf dem genannten Abschnitt bei Cisurupan, August 1980.*

Rechts: *Sturmgewölk braut sich über der CC 50 12 zusammen, als sie im August 1978 in Garut darauf wartet, den Frühpersonenzug nach Cikajang zu bespannen.*

Left: *The now-closed Garut – Cikajang section had grades as steep as 4% which meant hard work for the Mallets despite the short trains. Here a CC10 class 2-6-6-0 Mallet tank on the morning Cibatu – Cikajang train struggles uphill between Bayongbong and Cisurupan during August 1980.*

Right: *A beam of sunlight piercing the stormclouds above Garut highlights 2-6-6-0 Mallet no. CC 5012 which is waiting to work the morning train to Cikajang, August 1978.*

Beide GH

Bevor die Strecke von Tegal nach Prupuk 1981 verdieselt wurde, zogen die zerbrechlich wirkenden, aber gut unterhaltenen, B-Kuppler der Reihe B 52 die Züge. Hier fährt die B 52 03 im ersten Morgenlicht eines Augusttages 1978 mit dem 5.00h Zug aus einem Haltepunkt in Richtung Prupuk aus.

Until dieselization in 1981 the Tegal – Prupuk line was worked by the diminutive but well-maintained B52 class 0-4-0's. Here, the first rays of sunlight to pass beyond the trees catch B5203 as it makes an energetic start from a wayside halt with the 05.00 Tegal – Prupuk during August 1978.

GH

Im Scheinwerfer der im Bahnbetriebs-werk Cepu kalt abgestellten 1'C C5109 bricht sich an einem Augusttag 1978 die aufgehende Sonne.

The rising sun greets 2-6-0 C5109 slumbering inside Cepu shed during August 1978.

GH

Ländliche Szene in einem javanischen Kleinstadtbahnhof: Die Reisenden des 13.00h Zuges von Cepu nach Kradenan, der von der 2'C 2' Tenderlok C 28 30 geführt wird, steigen in einem Unterwegshalt in die bereitstehenden Pferdewagen um, Oktober 1975.

A typical Javan rural station scene: as a tropical storm brews up in the background, passengers from the 13.00 Cepu – Kradenan train hauled by C28 class 4-6-4 T no. 30 transfer to horse-drawn local transport at a stop en route, October 1975.

RM

Eine besondere Attraktion bot Indonesien durch den Einsatz uralter Loko-motiven auf einigen Nebenstrecken. Ein Sinnbild hierfür waren die holzge-feuerten 1'B Maschinen, die von Sharp Stewart zwischen 1880 und 1885 gebaut worden waren, und die, als etwa Hundertjährige, zu Beginn der 80er Jahre dieses Jahrhunderts noch immer Züge auf der Nebenstrecke von Madiun nach Slahung zogen. Hier vertreibt sich ein Junge in Ponorogo die Zeit mit Zuschauen, während bei der B 5012 das Feuer geschürt wird, August 1980.

One of the attractions of Indonesia for the railway enthusiast was the use of ancient equipment on some of the minor lines. This was typified by the wood-fired B50 class 2-4-0's built by Sharp Stewart in 1880 – 85 which, after some 100 years of service, were still hauling trains on the Madiun – Ponorogo – Slahung branch in the early 1980's. In this view a young boy passes his time by watching the fire being built up on B5012 at Ponorogo station during August 1980.

GH

Das Personal der B 5012 sieht wachsam in die hereinbrechende Dämmerung, während sie mit dem täglichen Personenzug von Madiun nach Slahung aus Ponorogo ausfahren, August 1980.

GH

The crew of B5012 looks intently into the gathering darkness as the daily Madiun–Slahung train heads away from Ponorogo at dusk, August 1980

Am indonesischen Nationalfeiertag 1978, dem 17. August, hält die passend beflaggte B 5012 mit ihrem Personenzug aus Slahung in der Hauptstraße von Madiun. Die alte schwarze Lok scheint in der grellbunten Straßenszene irgendwie fehl am Platz zu sein.

In 1978 on Indonesia's National Day, 17th August, a suitably beflagged B5012 pauses in one of Madiun's main streets with the train from Slahung. The old dark-painted locomotive seems curiously out of place in the bright bustling scene.

GH

Die untergehende Sonne findet gerade noch einmal ein Loch zwischen den Wolken, als eine D 52 1'D1' Madiun mit einem Güterzug in Richtung Surakarta verläßt, November 1978.

For just a moment the setting sun lying between horizon and clouds illuminates a D52 2-8-2 heading west from Madiun with an evening freight for Surakarta, November 1979.

HB

Wo einst das Feuer loderte, Bewegung und Leben herschte, ist nun alles kalt und leblos. Wuchernde Vegetation und feuchte Tropenluft nagen gemeinsam an den Rümpfen ausgemusterter Lokomotiven im Ausbesserungswerk Madiun, August 1978.

Where once there was fire, life and movement, now all is cold and still as creeping undergrowth and corrosive air compete to claim the carcasses of locomotives. Photographed at Madiun Workshops, August 1978.

GH

Zuckerfabrikbahnen (Pabrik Gula = PG). *Östlich von Tegal in Zentraljava überqueren die D-Kuppler 17 und 20 von der PG Sragi vorsichtig die PJKA Hauptstrecke. Zur Zeit der Aufnahme im August 1978 waren die Loks ölgefeuert, die Öltanks sind über den Kesseln zu sehen. Die Tender sind zum Schutz der ebenfalls verwendeten Bagasse mit Überdachungen ausgestattet.*

Sugar Factory (Pabrik Gula (PG)) Railways. *East of Tegal in Central Java the crews of PG Sragi 600 mm gauge 0-8-0's nos. 17 and 20 pose with their locomotives at a crossing over PJKA 1067 mm gauge track in August 1978. The tenders are fitted with covers for the storage of bagasse fuel, but the locomotives were at the time of this photograph oil-fired, the fuel oil tanks being mounted over the boilers.*

Bei Kediri in Ostjava gibt es mehrere Zuckerfabriken, die im Werksgelände, beziehungsweise auf den Feldern, Lokomotiven einsetzen. Abgebildet ist die BB Mallet-Tenderlok Nr. 224 mit 700 mm Spurweite im grasüberwucherten Rangierbahnhof der Zuckerfabrik Ngadiredjo. Die Bäume sind willkommene Schattenspender für die Arbeiter.

During August 1983 700 mm gauge oil-fired 0-4-4-0 Mallet tank no. 224 of PG Ngadiredjo hurries along the overgrown tracks of the railway's tree-lined shunting yard near Kediri, east Java. The function of the trees is to provide shade for the workers.

GH

Der klobige Öltank des D-Kupplers Nr. 6 der PG Wringinanom sticht in dieser Silhouette ins Auge, August 1986.

GH

0-8-0T no. 6 of PG Wringinanom heads into the sugar fields to pick up its load during August 1986. The rather incongruous fuel oil tank is very prominent in this silhouette.

Voll ins Zeug legen muß sich ein D-Kuppler der PG Wringinanom im August 1986 mit seiner Last. Dieses 700 mm Netz liegt in der Nähe von Situbondo in Ostjava.

An 0-8-0 tank locomotive of PG Wringinanom is seen here working hard as it hauls a long train of sugar cane in August 1986. This 700 mm gauge system is situated near Situbondo at the eastern end of Java.

GH

Die Abendsonne wirft einen kräftigen Schein auf die kleine B1' Lokomotive der Zuckerfabrik De Maas, in der Nähe von Situbondo gelegen, als sie mit ihrer süßen Fracht an Palmen und Tabakfeldern vorbei auf die Fabrik zufährt, August 1986.

GH

Heading home to the mill with a load of cane at the end of another day's work, PG De Maas 700 mm gauge 0-4-2 tender-tank locomotive no. 1 passes through a peaceful tropical scene basking in the rich light of the low evening sun. Photographed near Situbondo in August 1986.